**Books by Phillip D. Cortez**

Night Rhythms

When I Close My Eyes/Al cerrar mis ojos

Ava & The Monsters

Pancakes For Dinner!

Pizza For Breakfast!

# #TheHappyManifesto
## Three Rules for Happier Students

Phillip D. Cortez, MCM

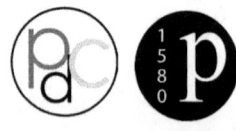

Copyright © 2018 Phillip D. Cortez

All rights reserved. No part of this book may be used or reproduced in any manner without the express written permission of the author except in the case of brief quotations embodied in critical articles or reviews.

Published by 1580 Publishing
Printed in the United States of America.

ISBN: 978-0-9964623-9-6
Library of Congress Number: 2018911912

Visit www.phillipcortez.com to book your school visits, literacy nights and organizational team building activites, workshops and other speaking engagements.

This manifesto is dedicated to all teachers, coaches, caseworkers, therapists and parents of children all over the world. Thank you so much for the incredible work you do!

This guide is about ways or strategies we can use in our every day lives and share with our students and children. The following should not be considered a substitute for professional care. If you or someone you know is in need of someone to talk to, please call the National Suicide Prevention Hotline: 1-800-273-8255.

For my wife, Patty, and our beautiful children Ivan, Cameron, Ava & Zoe. You provide me with all of the happiness I could ever ask for.

# Contents

**The First Rule of Happiness:**
Always Be Better Than "Good"

**The Second Rule of Happiness:**
Work Hard For The Dream
(Understanding the Dream vs the Fantasy)

**The Third Rule of Happiness:**
Fostering the Dreams of Others
(You never know when you're going to need help!)

**Putting It All Together**

**Acknowledgments**

# Introduction

It wasn't the boy's wrinkled, yellow school polo that looked (and smelled) like it had been taken out of the hamper or his finger combed hair that I noticed first. It wasn't even the dried toothpaste residue on the side of his mouth that he forgot to completely wipe away when getting ready for school.

It was his eyes.

As young as this boy was – I think he was in third or fourth grade – I could sense that those blue-gray eyes had seen a lot, or at least more than a young boy that age should. They were hesitant, moving around in a continuous cycle, scanning the room for laughing kids, perhaps. First side to side, then back to me, then to the ground at his untied shoe.

When words finally escaped his mouth, I could hear the shyness, the apprehension, in his small voice.

"Were you afraid to walk home alone from the

bus stop?" he asked, referring to a line from my second picture book, *When I Close My Eyes*. The boy in the story is depicted walking alone on a spooky path amongst barren and hollow trees.

"Because I'm afraid of walking home alone," he said.

I struggled to find the right words in that moment, as I stared back at him. His eyes grew moist and I could tell that a tear would roll down his cheek if he blinked too hard. He wanted to know why I wrote that line, to see if I, too, had been bullied as a kid. The librarian at the school later confirmed to me that this boy and his siblings were living in hard conditions and that Child Protective Services ran periodic welfare checks on the family. We had a conversation about how kids could be mean, especially to those kids who are different – like this boy.

Up until this encounter, the concept of following

*#TheHappyManifesto - Three Rules for Happier Students*

three rules in order to be happy was something I used as material for school presentations. I developed this concept because I didn't want to turn my school visits into glorified book sales. If you ask any librarian or teacher who has hired me to speak at their campus, I hate selling my books during my visits because it's awkward for me to pivot from author to salesman (The last thing I need is to get sidetracked during an important discussion on writing to fourth grade students with the realization that I might not have enough change to break a twenty dollar bill).

No, I wanted these presentations to be more than read-out-louds followed by the typical Q&A session. I wanted to add something of value. And the more schools I began to visit, the more I began to identify more students just like the boy with the sad, blue-gray eyes. As a result, the concept of happiness became more and more important. My message about happiness began to evolve with every school visit until I made it official and began calling the discussion, The Three Rules to

Happiness. Once that happened, something amazing occurred: My books and read-out-louds started taking a back seat to my discussion on The Three Rules of Happiness. Suddenly, I found myself weaving the stories into the "happy" talks. What used to be filler material now took center stage.

Now, I happen to know that schools everywhere are doing a great job of teaching our kids by raising awareness about the impacts that bullying can have. This teaching is reinforced at home and in the community. But are we doing enough?

I ask the question because it appears that as much as we seem to be teaching our kids about bullying, as much as we see and hear anti-bullying campaigns at the local and national level, there are still tragic stories that come across our news feeds. Have we become numb to these important anti-bullying messages? And what about these tragic stories? There was a time when they used to hit home and cut us to the core. Today, the scroll of a finger on a social media timeline helps us avoid the cut and the eventual scar.

In my opinion, the tragic stories of bullied kids that eventually committed suicide or hurt others are becoming too common; perhaps we just can't keep up with them. Or just maybe the whole concept of bullying is so common that it has become the norm. Trust me, I'm not here to take a position on mental healthcare, the Second Amendment or anything political. But this is what we know: School and workplace violence happen far too often in the United States. And while the blueprint for why these tragedies happen is up for debate, we should agree on this: Long before the first bullet was shot (or the first weapon bought), there was someone who became lost for some reason. That person lacked emotional (and sometimes clinical) support, hope and empathy from others when they probably needed it the most.

What if we could apply a strategy that would not

only help strengthen our own sense of self-worth and happiness but the children we teach, too?

## About The Rules

I am not a doctor or expert in these things. However, I am a father helping to raise four children. And it doesn't take years of schooling to conclude that we're looking at a happiness shortage these days. This is why I decided to take my Three Rules To Happiness discussion and turn it into a book (or manifesto, if you will). In the spirit of simplifying a topic that can be easily complex, my goal is to offer a different perspective with simple and common sense approaches to provide our kids with a foundation to being happier people. Whether you're a teacher or parent (or both) we can all apply these rules to better our children's lives.

The Three Rules work in tandem with each other; we should look at them holistically. But the key word is **simple**. Once again, anyone can follow these rules! It doesn't matter where you fall on the political spectrum, your ethnicity, socioeconomic status, social status, religious views, sexuality, gender, age or geography.

    This little boy who approached me after a school presentation gave me more of a purpose than he ever realized. I often think about him. He'd be close to middle school age now. He reminded me of another blue-eyed boy I grew up and went to school with who was picked on every day after class. Kids lined up to fight him for the hell of it. And the older kids watched it all go down.

    It happened at the bus top.

    I never helped my old classmate out back then, either because I was too much of a wimp or scared of getting my butt kicked, too. And even though I was just a kid at the time, I had a voice. I could have said something, told someone. But I didn't. Who was going to listen to me anyway? I mean, even some of the teachers at school weren't so nice to him. I suppose in the end it's easier to do nothing than get your hands dirty. And that school of thought is just flat out unacceptable; I've always regretted not speaking up.

In some way, I hope this book can help make it up to him...

# The First Rule of Happiness

*#TheHappyManifesto - Three Rules for Happier Students*

The First Rule of Happiness is the most important rule because it's the ultimate table-setter. If we were building a house together, and if you've ever seen a home under construction, the First Rule would be that foundational slab with all the pipes sticking out of it. I'll be referring to the First Rule as we move forward and cover the remaining two because I want to show you how it all starts to come together. There's a method to the madness, so to speak.

I like to make it a point to carefully watch the students file into the library or auditorium whenever I get the opportunity to visit a campus. In fact, I can usually tell whether it's going to be a good session or not before they even finish taking their seats (Criss-cross applesauce…). I stand there and smile just to see what kind of reaction I'm going to get. Some kids look at me confused while others smile. And every fifth kid in line or so, I ask the same question:

"How are you doing?"

With very few exceptions, the answer is almost always the same. It doesn't matter where I am, what side of the tracks I'm on, whether it's an elementary school or a high school. Ninety-nine percent of the time I get the default, go-to, don't-even-have-to-think-about-it answer:

"Good."

Think about how you go about your day and the same question is posed to you. How are you responding? It's normally that canned answer we rely on. And when you think about it, so is the question: *How you doin?* or *How's it going?* It's become the way we say hello, right? In the UK, you hear something similar: *You all right?*

Asking someone how they're doing is our way of socially doing our part so that people don't get the wrong impression of us. Now we can move along with our day with clean consciences.

It's the one question I can ask while passing

someone on the sidewalk and totally expect (and be satisfied with) the question directed right back at me without either one of us stopping.

"How's it going, Robbie?"

"How's t going, Phil?"

Two questions. No answers.

And nobody's honest. I mean, how many of us actually expect a meaningful response to that question in the first place?

"Hey, Joe, how's it going?"

"Thanks for asking, Jim, I'm feeling pretty lonely and vulnerable right now…"

But let's focus on the answer. The word "good" is not "great." At the same time it's not "Terrible." It's just, well, it's okay. Whatever (Or as the kids say, *whatevs*). One thing I ask students to do when we're talking about this is to give the word "good" a grade the way a teacher would grade your paper. The majority of kids give it a C. Think about what a C was when you were going to school. It was Satisfactory, which was a more proper way to say that it was *average*.

## The First Rule of Happiness:
## Always be better than *good*.

More than anything, the First Rule is an attitude adjustment. If the word "good" is a nice way of saying "average," than we have a lot of work to do in helping students (and adults) understand how valuable they really are; some people do not know their self worth – and it's priceless!

I make it a point to let these students know that as I scan across auditoriums and libraries when this topic is discussed, I tell them: I see your faces and I do not see average!

That's when we start over; I ask the audience a second time: How are you doing? This time, they are challenged to provide a different response. As a result the students can't raise their hands fast enough. I hear all kinds of responses: Excellent, awesome, outstanding, magnificent, bodacious, wonderful, fantastic, groovy (yes, a kid really said it), and even some made up words (fantastical, greaterrific). The whole point of this exercise is to help kids understand that we shouldn't just settle for being *good*. Bananas are good.

We have to strive to be better than good, not only in school, but in everything that we do – and that includes how we treat each other. We just need to adjust our attitudes a little bit. Don't just show up, be an active participant. Don't settle for mediocrity; raise your expectation levels. You get the idea.

*Phillip D. Cortez, MCM*

> **Activity**: If the word *good* is another word for average, what are some stronger words we can use that would set the bar higher for ourselves? See how many you can come up with in the space provided.

#TheHappyManifesto - *Three Rules for Happier Students*

There's a reason why I tell students and teachers that this is the First Rule of Happiness. Because every rule feeds off of each other, we should consider the First Rule of Happiness as the rule that helps set the table. After all, we can't eat dinner unless we set the table first, right? Okay, if you're family is like mine, sometimes we bypass the table and opt for the couch, but still.

So now that we know the rule, let's take a look at how we can apply this as parents, teachers, coaches, etc. And I'll use myself as an example.

You see, I was the kid that ALWAYS forgot to put his name on his paper in school. It got to the point that when teachers passed out the graded homework, they just knew that nameless paper was mine. One teacher made it a point to get theatrical about it.

"Oh boy, what do we have here?" she gasped aloud, channeling her inner Harvey Feirstein. "I wonder whose THIS paper belongs to?" The teacher pinched the top-right corner of the homework assignment and dangled it arm's length away as if it was a dirty diaper.

In dramatic fashion the teacher would slowly approach my desk, by this time the class knew it was me, and the public shaming would ensue.

"I just have no clue whose paper this could be, class!" she'd scream looking right at me. "It's a shame that I had to take ten points off of an A paper because someone was so careless as to not put his name on it!"

Man, I hated when she did that. But given all the hard times I gave teachers as a student from Kindergarten to my senior year in high school, I probably deserved harsher treatment. ;)

The truth of the matter was this: I was so focused on getting down to business and tackling the assignment (and probably trying to be one of the first to finish so that I could goof off), I skipped the most important and basic step in the entire process. It's like a no-brainer – everyone knows that you're supposed to put your name on your work, whether it's homework as a student, those lesson plans as a teacher or that spreadsheet at the office.

Sadly, it wasn't until my freshman year in high school that I finally broke my ridiculous habit of not putting my name on my assignments (and mind you, this didn't happen all the time). My English teacher, a wonderful man by the name of Robert Candelaria, explained why it's so important to put your name on your work. And his explanation has always stayed with me.

He explained that our names have a meaning. Important people gave us our names. And when we put our names on our assignments, all the work, all the responses and all the effort is a direct reflection of us (I know, a little deep, but it was Catholic school, so...).

I have taken Mr. Candelaria's lesson a step further and have integrated it into my talks with students of all ages and employees at various organizations. We're all going to make mistakes; that's inevitable (and the reason why there's an eraser on the other end of the pencil, right?). We're all going to overlook a few details on that spreadsheet. Putting our names on something and understanding that the contents that follow is a reflection of our work, well, that's us following the First Rule; we're being better than good.

This is a lesson that all students can follow. And it doesn't matter what grade the student is in. When we're better than good, we place a higher emphasis on quality work. When quality becomes a part of who we are, we will cut down on potential mistakes and oversights. Students slow down, take their time and aren't in such a rush to complete an assignment (like yours truly used to be).

When speaking to students about this, I let the kids in on a little secret: I tell them that their teachers can see an A+ paper before they even read the answers. All the teachers seem to nod in agreement. That A+ paper is neatly written. The student clearly shows how the answer was found. Teachers can tell when a student took time on the assignment. Oh, and there's a name on it.

Conversely, teachers can eyeball the bad grades just by looking at the paper that was turned in. They can see when a student began the assignment five minutes before the bell rang, most-likely because the writing is barely legible and sentences are as incomplete as the entire assignment.

"How many of you have turned in an incomplete homework assignment because you thought it was better than turning in nothing at all?" I ask students. Brave kids raise their hands.

"But if our work is a reflection of us, what does an incomplete assignment say about us? Are we, too, incomplete?"

When we are better than good, we double check our work and avoid shortcuts, I tell students, especially older kids. As an example, I talk about my first children's book, Night Rhythms. Even though it is a simple rhyming book for little kids, I get a big kick out of reading for adults, too, mainly because I like to see their reactions. But towards the end of the book, the little boy in the story, beautifully illustrated by my high school buddy, Marco Saenz, is depicted standing on his tippy toes in front of an open fridge as he reaches for a slice of chocolate cake.

This is where I tell the audience that as awesome as I love this illustration, I almost missed a mistake. You see, the illustration did not coincide with the text of the story. The original text went like this:

*Tip, toe. Tippety toe,*

*As I sneak outside my room,*

*Slip and slide go my feet on the cold kitchen tile,*

*There's some chocolate cake in the fridge…*

Marco's illustration showed the boy barefoot. As much as I loved that illustration (still do), I knew deep inside that it's hard to slip and slide on tile a la Tom Cruise in the movie *Risky Business* when you're not wearing socks. And when I share this insight with students, I tell them that I could have let it go. I could have let it slide (you see what I did there?). And even though only a handful of readers would pick up on this, I would always know that I cut a corner in order to meet a deadline.

I use the analogy of when we have a rock in our shoe. We can still walk, heck we could probably still run, but we'd feel it with every step. In my case, I would feel that annoyance every time I read the words on that page in front of a group of people, probably wondering whether the audience would notice the disconnect.

How did I fix my problem? Better yet, how did I apply the First Rule of Happiness and be better than good? Rather than having Marco make changes to the illustration (I love those little toes in that picture), I opted to change the text instead. The version everyone knows now goes like this:

> *Tip, toe. Tippety toe,*
>
> *As I sneak outside my room,*
>
> *Pitter pat go my feet on the cold kitchen tile,*
>
> *There's some chocolate cake in the fridge…*

Problem solved. Deadline met. Plus, I have a great example to share with audiences to further illustrate my point.

The beauty behind this first rule is that we can apply it to so many facets of our lives, starting with our attitudes. We have to have a positive attitude if we want to start any assignment, any work project. When we apply the First Rule of being better than good, students begin to think twice about practicing bad habits. Professionals go the extra mile for their clients. And when I begin my talks to both students and employees, I can't stress enough how important it is to have a strong, positive attitude.

One of my connections on Linkedin posted a great picture of a teacher in front of a dry erase board. Even though there are many versions of this picture all over the Internet, it still bears sharing here. Plus, this makes for a great idea for a workshop group activity.

The premise of the photo was to illustrate that even though it takes **Hard Work, Skills** and **Knowledge** to do a great job, having a great attitude is 100% essential:

**Let each letter of the alphabetic has a value equals to it sequence of the alphabetical order:**

| A | B | C | D | E | F | G | H | I | J | K | L | M | N | O | P | Q | R | S | T | U | V | W | X | Y | Z |
|---|---|---|---|---|---|---|---|---|---|---|---|---|---|---|---|---|---|---|---|---|---|---|---|---|---|
| 1 | 2 | 3 | 4 | 5 | 6 | 7 | 8 | 9 | 10 | 11 | 12 | 13 | 14 | 15 | 16 | 17 | 18 | 19 | 20 | 21 | 22 | 23 | 24 | 25 | 26 |

| S K I L L S  <br> 19 11 9 12 12 19 | = | 82 |
|---|---|---|
| K N O W L E D G E <br> 11 14 15 23 12 5 4 7 5 | = | 96 |
| H A R D   W O R K <br> 8 1 12 4   23 15 18 11 | = | 98 |
| A T T I T U D E <br> 1 20 20 9 20 21 4 5 | = | 100 |

We all know that having a positive attitude can lead to positive outcomes. But I want to share a story about someone who displayed a very negative attitude recently. I was watching my beloved Oakland Athletics take on the Houston Astros in a 4-game series last July when I saw something that fans don't normally see.

Astros closer Ken Giles was pulled in the ninth inning after giving up three runs without recording an out. Houston's manager, AJ Hinch, had seen enough and took Giles out of the game. That's when Giles reportedly cursed at his manager as he walked off the mound to the dugout. Giles allegedly directed an F-bomb at Hinch.

Now in fairness, we see players lose their cool on the field and on the court all the time. As fans we have come to appreciate the passion that these world-class athletes display night after night in an effort to chase a championship. This type of passion can be channeled in a positive way. Teammates, coaches and fans feed off of it, excitement builds and the energy can be electric.

But there's a downside to this passion, especially when it becomes destructive. Giles, clearly frustrated, demonstrated a lack of control (physically and mentally) and displayed a terrible attitude in front of a huge audience. And that audience most definitely included children. Houston would not only demote Giles the very next day, sending him to their Triple A affiliate in Fresno, but the organization would end up trading him to Toronto a few weeks later. Now Giles has to start all over and prove himself to new teammates and a new manager.

For those students reading this, we have to be able to learn from moments like these and apply them in our own lives. Things aren't always going to go our way.

Let's contrast the story above with what happened to New York Giants quarterback Eli Manning during the 2017-18 season. As the face of the franchise since 2014 (which included two Super Bowl victories),

Manning was unceremoniously benched in what would turn out to be a completely botched operation by the team's front office. The move by the team was seen as classless, as a bewildered and even emotional Eli Manning was left to answer questions from the media.

Now let me be totally transparent here: I do not like the New York Giants. I am a Dallas Cowboys fan. And as much as I have yelled at my television, urging defenders to take Manning down or make him so uncomfortable that he tosses three interceptions en route to a Cowboys victory, I actually have a lot of respect for him. A LOT.

You see, if there was ever a moment where he could have pulled rank, vented, thrown his weight around, gone on a media blitz denouncing the unpopular benching, well, everyone would have totally understood. But rather than play it out this way, Manning chose to rise above that noise and accept the demotion with dignity, saying that he would comply with what was a team decision, albeit a decision that should have been much better organized and executed.

Before he was benched, Manning owned a consecutive games started streak that began in Week 11 of the 2004 season. Apparently, management gave Manning the option of starting for a series and then get benched so that the streak could remain active.

"My feeling is that if you are going to play the other guys, play them," he was quoted as saying. "Starting just to keep the streak going and knowing that you won't finish the game and have a chance to win is pointless to me, and it tarnishes the streak. Like I always have, I will be ready to play if and when needed."

The class that Manning demonstrated during this very rough point in his career won over this Cowboys fan, which is saying a lot. The point is that we all have a choice to make when we're met with adversity of some kind. For students we face it in the classroom and the playground.

In our professional lives it seems that we are facing more and more adversity these days, whether it's in the office or even on our social media timelines. We get round-the-clock emails that keep us within the scopes of our employment nearly 24-7. All of this has become the norm.

As an exercise, let's think about the times we may have handled an adverse situation with a fellow teacher, student or administrator the wrong way. What could you have done differently? When you replay the events on that projection screen inside your head, how does the story unfold? What do you do? What do you say?

Whenever I go back in time and wonder how things would be if I chose a better way to resolve a problem, I go back to Kindergarten – to the time that I got my first (sort of) kiss and my first paddling on the same day. Not many people can accomplish this, but somehow I found a way.

First the good: A first grader – I'll spare her the embarrassment and just say her name was Claire – sat next to me on the school bus and made her way over to my seat. I was pretty nervous, as this was my first day of school and riding the bus for the first time. I don't recall every detail but here's what I know: I could smell the cherry lip balm shortly before her lips met mine. That's when I heard a chorus of yelling, as all the kids near us began to holler. But that's not how I got in trouble (I just thought it'd be cool to brag about that kiss).

No, I got in trouble later that morning, as the teacher was playing music from the Disney cartoon, Peter and the Wolf. This kid – his name was Todd – wouldn't sit still. To this day, Sergei Prokofiev's musical score to this cartoon brings me back to that classroom, that dusty chalkboard and the smell of crayons and fresh Big Chief tablet paper.

Todd was determined to ruin the experience for everyone, as our teacher warned him that more outbursts would put an end to the fun. I wanted to tell him to sit still. I also wanted to tell him to shut up.

Shut up. Sit still.

Todd broke the silence again with his hyperactivity. This time I was going to say something. I was going to tell him to shut up! And sit still!

"SHIT STILL!"

As you can imagine, all the kids freaked out. My teacher heard it all and promptly sent me to the principal's office. In what was surely the fastest fall from grace in school history – one minute the kissing Casanova of Kindergarten, a potty-mouthed rebel the next. And I could have helped my cause by apologizing, by explaining how it was an accident and that I mixed up my words, how Shut and Sit sort of came out at the same time. Maybe I would have avoided that wooden paddle stinging my behind like a thousand bees. Maybe.

Instead I chose to talk back, deny and stonewall.

*#TheHappyManifesto - Three Rules for Happier Students*

In a court of law I'd be considered a hostile witness. I even talked back to the teacher. This is why I was sent to the office on my first day of school. It's how a man by the name of Carol T. Welch - that name alone just *sounded* like it carried the wrath of justice with it - took out a thin paddle from his desk drawer and held it like it was sacred. He had me lean against his desk and stare out his window. All I saw were cars whizzing by on Alameda Street and the sound of kids playing in the schoolyard. I vividly remember wishing to be one of those kids, playing in the playground at that very moment instead of…

SMACK!! *Eyes closed tightly. Tears forming. Sharp sting radiating from that special spot where the glutes and hamstrings meet. Suck. It. Up.

The walk back to class was almost as tough as getting paddled by the principal. It was a true walk of shame, as I was faced with having to go back to class and face my classmates and feel their stares. I was now the kid with baggage, the student that all the kids would talk about to their parents after school. I could just imagine how those dinner conversations may have gone.

"How was school, son? Anything exciting happen today?"

"This one kid made out with a girl and then lost his mind, cursed out the teacher like a straight up G and got smacked around by the principal. The teacher tried to calm the situation by playing classical music. Other than that it was ok, for a Monday."

Attitude. Is. Everything. A good one can help us and, as I've clearly shown, a bad one can certainly hurt us. Like former Houston Astros pitcher Ken Giles had to start fresh with a new team, I had to try and start fresh with my teacher and my classmates.

The First Rule of Happiness, when we're better than good, automatically checks our attitudes; we're in a mindset in which ordinary or average is not good enough. We quickly realize that it can be applied in all aspects of our lives, not just the classroom or in an office setting. We can be better than good to our neighbors, our friends and even strangers. Suddenly we begin treating people with respect. We have the ability to have more empathy towards others, especially those in need of some kind of support or help.

You see, a happier classroom has to start with ourselves as parents and educators. Applying that First Rule for ourselves is a critical first step if we want to extend it to our children. And when we encourage them to apply this First Rule, they will soon set that higher standard for themselves. More importantly, they can expect that standard from other classmates around them.

As important as it is for students to be better than good to everyone around them, they have to realize that they must be better than good to themselves, too. Now I know that maybe this sounds selfish. But think about it: How can we be better than good to other people, how do we begin to respect and have empathy for others, if we don't have respect and self-love for ourselves?

For example, I have always tried to stay in shape, mainly because I played a number of sports growing up all the way through high school. And after my schooling I tried staying in somewhat good shape, mainly because I didn't want to let myself go and suffer the scrutiny from my friends (who can be relentless). However, the older I became, the more I kept taking my health for granted.

The wakeup call came on my 36th birthday. It was the day my father had to go to the hospital because he couldn't stop shivering, couldn't catch his breath. A chest x-ray at the hospital confirmed that he had pneumonia. With treatment, my dad would be okay. Unfortunately, that chest x-ray also showed a spot on my father's lung. My dad would lose his battle with cancer in 2014, two days before my 38th birthday.

This is when I made the decision to start taking my health more seriously. Rather than just trying to appease my own ego, I decided that I was going to focus on feeling great, instead. That meant working from the inside out and not the other way around. I'd begin to start closely examining what I was going to eat and when I was going to eat. I adopted a vegetarian (sometimes vegan) diet. In addition, I began investing more of my time in the gym, working out smarter, focusing on my heart and conditioning rather than an improved physique.

Am I trying to fight Father Time? Sure, who isn't? But my absolute driving force is the memory of the day I sat next to my father's bed a few months before he died – he was no longer sleeping in his regular bed and now had a hospital bed installed in his bedroom – and we were watching a Monday Night Football game. My daughter Zoe, who was about three years old at the time, bounced into the room to say hello. Three-year-olds can be loud and my father wasn't feeling well that night. So I sent her downstairs, in which she happily obliged in her carefree way.

The look on my father's face as he watched her has never left me. Tears streamed down his cheeks and he looked helpless. I buried my face in his chest and cried. I felt just as helpless as he must have. I mean, what can you say in that moment? I just cried with him.

"I wish I had more time," he said.

I could hear the beating of his heart and feel his chest rise up and down with every breath, ebbing and flowing like the tide. It was soothing, like when I was a kid and I'd sit on his lap in the evenings, falling asleep to that same ebb and flow of his breathing. I felt safe in those moments.

Looking back, even as I write this, I still marvel at how during one of the lowest points in his life, as helpless as he was feeling at that moment, my father still managed to make me feel better – just by breathing.

I want to offer this same type of comfort to my children, too. The loss of my father forced me to think about my own mortality. A lot of my friends started having children during their twenty-something years while I waited until I was in my 30's. What kind of legacy would I leave my own children and, if I'm lucky, my grandchildren one day?

Ultimately, this is why I upped the ante, so to speak, from a fitness standpoint. Will this perspective prevent cancer or other long-term, life-threatening illnesses down the road? There are no guarantees in life, right? But if there's one thing I know a little something about from my marketing days, it's about positioning. And I am now positioning myself in a healthier way, thus, giving myself a fighting chance should I ever get bad news from the doctor.

Applying the First Rule in this case has certainly helped me from a fitness standpoint. However, it's also allowing my children to benefit, as well. Every minute I spend investing in my own personal health is buying me more time with them as I get older. That means more performances, more recitals, more games, more laughs, more tears, more lessons learned.

More memories.

*#TheHappyManifesto - Three Rules for Happier Students*

**Activity (Part 1)**: On this page (or a separate sheet of paper), have the class or your child list every single person that truly matters most in their lives. These are the people that drive you, inspire you and add incredible value to you.

**Activity (Part 2)**: Have students explain why these people made it onto their lists. They might write words such as, *dependable, loyal, love of my life,* etc. Have them take some time with this part.

When you and your students are finished with the Why part of this exercise, have them take a look at that list for a few moments and read what they wrote. Encourage them to share some of those awesome qualities owned by the people they identified. Ask them to say a little something about the people that bring these awesome qualities to their lives. I'm willing to bet that each and every quality written down was better than good, right? At no point would you ever see the word average. Right?

Right.

When students see those words, those special qualities that these people possess, we can help make them realize that they, too, can be those qualities in return. That's right. *Be* those qualities.

I encourage teachers and parents to take part in this activity, as well. For anyone who was dependable or always there for you, strive to exemplify those same qualities in return. You can start by applying The First Rule for each of those people you just listed on that sheet of paper. And when you (and your students and children) start to extend that radius to people who weren't on the list, that's when the magic starts to happen.

# The Second Rule of Happiness

*#TheHappyManifesto - Three Rules for Happier Students*

How many of you dream about winning the lottery? Seriously, you're reading this right now and I am willing to bet that the large majority of people (if not all) would love to win the lottery, especially if it was a record Powerball win.

This is a question I often ask parents and teachers in live environments and workshop settings. And, of course, all hands are usually raised because, come on, who wouldn't want to get their hands on all that dough, right?

But then I follow up the question with another: How many of you actually buy the ticket? A good two-thirds of the hands go down, some more slowly than others along with nervous laughter scattered throughout the room. This is one of the ways I transition to my Second Rule of Happiness, a rule that requires us to understand the difference between fantasy and reality. It's about dreams. More importantly, as Rudyard Kipling wrote, it's about not making dreams our masters.

*Phillip D. Cortez, MCM*

# The Second Rule of Happiness: Always Work Hard To Follow Your Dreams

I know people who are still waiting for their BIG BREAK, waiting for a star to fall or that ship to come in. And while some people are born under a lucky star, the vast majority of successful and accomplished people worked very hard to get to where they are. These people endured sleepless nights, time spent away from family, working multiple jobs to make ends meet and sacrificed daily so that they could achieve their dreams.

As a writer, I always tell kids that the art of writing is actually re-writing. I let them know that they, too, are writers, because the steps in the Writer's Workshop that they are learning in class are the very same steps that I and many other writers out there are incorporating into our professional lives. There are outlines to make, thinking maps to create out of brainstorm sessions, drafts to write and share with our peers.

For me, on top of all of the above, I have to do my work in smaller windows of time than most people. As I type this sentence there is a puppy I have to keep an eye on, especially when he starts sniffing around the living room carpet. There are my children who wander aimlessly into the room and I swear that they're playing a game with each other to see how many questions they can ask before I flip out or cry (whichever comes first).

Then, of course, I have to fight a battle of having a shorter attention span than most – SQUIRREL!

What was I saying? Oh…

I realize, of course, that not all students want to be writers when they grow up. In fact, many third and fourth grade students I speak to absolutely do not like to write. And that's okay. I make it a point to let them know that everyone's dream is as unique as they are. I've heard it all, from doctors and lawyers to zookeepers and professional athletes. One kid loved working with clay and wanted to become an animator (which I thought was totally cool).

No matter what that dream might be – it's okay if they don't know what that dream is yet, either - our students can't just sit there and wait for that dream to come true. Following their dreams means working hard for them, failing but still getting up off of the mat to keep trying.

Understanding the fantasy and the reality is as simple as wanting to win the lottery (the fantasy) without buying the ticket (the effort). We have to know the difference between the two. The fantasy is a unicorn or a flying pig. No matter the type of audience, I tell them that there are individuals out there who are much older than I am that are still waiting… and waiting for opportunity to come knocking on their doors. Meanwhile, others are knocking down doors, working hard at their crafts, learning from mistakes. They're getting better - better than good.

You didn't think that just because we moved onto

The Second Rule that we'd forget about The First Rule, right? After all, it's pretty tough to apply one without incorporating the other into our daily lives somehow. This is what makes these rules so easy to follow - they stick to one another like the gum underneath the desks in your classrooms! (Sorry... not sorry).

In this sense these two rules are closely related in that if students don't follow The First Rule, there's a pretty solid chance that they will not apply The Second Rule. Hard work goes out the window if they can't be better than average, merely just getting by. No goal can be reached if there's no real effort behind it.

Think of the job you happen to be at right now and the people you work with. Understanding that we all have different work ethics, think of the person that just does enough to skate by or, even worse, takes shortcuts at every opportunity. Yet somehow, these are the same people that expect high praise, right? I'll bet you're picturing that person right now. It's okay, you can curse out loud. I won't hear you.

These are the people that spend more time circumventing (and understanding) the system and working their way around HR policies and procedures than they know about their own jobs. In short, they are good at getting away with not working. These are the people that become unhappy when others succeed or get praised for doing a good job and being counted on. For some reason, these people have an axe to grind. And nine times out of ten, they are unhappy at how transparent they are.

These people are the ones that gave up on their dreams. And they are unhappy because they probably expected so much more out of their lives.

I am willing to bet that if the person you are thinking about had a reboot, an opportunity to rewrite his or her career (or life) script, you would not see this person at work anymore. This person would be doing something else, something more fulfilling.

Want to know the sad irony behind all of this? The person you're thinking about right now has every opportunity available to totally start all over and rewrite that script. But it takes work. They'll always be stuck if they do not apply the Second Rule of Happiness. Working hard for the dream means not giving up even when the world seems to be falling down. That good 'ol first rule sets the table for us from an attitude standpoint; it helps us stay positive.

Okay, so now that we've thought about that annoying co-worker, let's do a little self-reflection. I know, this could be a tough pill to swallow for some of us but when it comes to happiness, you cannot fake it. Let me repeat that: true happiness cannot be faked. It starts from within and spreads like wildfire. In the last chapter we learned how important it was for us to be better than good to ourselves, that self-love is important, right? Well part of self-love means looking in the mirror and being honest with ourselves, too.

So here we go. I just described that coworker and we went into some detail at how they make life miserable for us. Now we need to ask ourselves a very important question:

Could I be that person, too?

Now, I'm not saying that you're a terrible person. But are you guilty of giving up on your dream (and taking it out on others)? Are you working in a career that you always dreamed of working in? If you had the opportunity to reboot, if you could re-write your script, how would it read?

As you think of these answers, never forget this very important truth: There's still time to rewrite that script. But it's not a magic pill you can take or a star you can wish upon. It comes with applying The First and Second Rules of Happiness.

So why are we doing this, you might be asking? I know, this is about our students, not parents and teachers, right? Right. But it all starts with us. We have to lead by example here. In fact, this is a critical teaching moment for us as parents and educators. We now have the opportunity to teach our students that sometimes the problems they have with other kids, those moments of conflict that lead to petty arguments one day, a schoolyard fight the next (or worse) can be squashed when we teach them a little self-reflection first.

Here are some of these greatest hits we've all come to love over the years from our students:

- It's the teacher's fault for that bad grade...
- It wasn't my fault, I got in trouble because he was making me laugh...
- She always gives us too much homework...

I can go on but you get the idea: This little self-reflection exercise helps teach our kids a little lesson about accountability.

Here is just a small sample of positive outcomes that arise when we teach our kids how to self-reflect:

- They slow down, becoming less impulsive...
- They are not so quick to judge...
- They begin to think about outcomes or consequences before they take action...
- They start taking ownership of the decisions they make...

It's not easy for a person to learn that they might be the problem. It's hard. But when we're better than good and when we work hard instead of wishing, these obstacles don't seem so tough to navigate around. When our students understand that this kind of self-reflection is all a part of their growth and potential, it clears the path for them to reach their goals.

Ultimately, this self-reflection helps them to see life through a different lens, one that gives them another perspective.

*#TheHappyManifesto - Three Rules for Happier Students*

One of the stories I like to share when talking about The First and Second Rules is a story my mother told me about two brothers who followed two very different paths.

The older brother is a highly successful businessman. He's won numerous awards for being an entrepreneur and has been recognized for his charitable work. In the story, a newspaper is attempting to do a write up on this successful man's latest achievement. But while researching the story, the reporter decides to find the successful man's younger brother for a quote.

Once the reporter locates the younger brother, the reporter is in disbelief at how different these two men are. While the older brother is a success in every way, the younger brother is the complete opposite. He's scraggly looking; one would even say that he looked sickly. The younger brother couldn't hold down a steady job, drifting like a peace of wood that the tide brings in. As far as anyone can tell, the only consistency with this man is that he sits in the same stool at the same bar on most nights.

At an almost complete loss for words, the reporter finally asks, "How are you and your older brother so different?"

The younger brother rubs his stubbly face and thinks for a moment. He then takes a sip of his drink and finally responds.

"It's all because of my father," he began. "He was hard on me, his expectations were high and he just kept pushing me because he thought I wasn't good enough."

After leaving the younger brother, the reporter then met with the older, successful brother. The interview, as expected, went well. But before the reporter left the older brother's office, she asked one last question, almost like an afterthought.

"How did you become so successful?" the reporter asked.

The older, successful brother thought about it for a moment, smiled and then responded.

"It's all because of my father," the older brother said. "He was hard on me. He had high expectations. And he was always pushing me to be better. And he did it because he believed in me."

We can see the first two rules coming into play in this story. The successful brother was pushed to be better than average. He was able to understand that his father meant well and wanted the best possible outcomes for his son. So he worked hard as a result. The successful brother worked hard for the dream.

The story also provides us a lesson about perspective. Here you had two brothers that took very different paths. Both brothers shared the same father, the same upbringing and the same expectations yet they had different perspectives. And different perspectives can produce different outcomes.

**Activity**:

- Raise your right arm up and stick your thumb up as if you were hitchhiking.

- Now slowly move that right arm in a circular, clockwise motion (12 o'clock, 3 o'clock, etc.). Good!

- Slowly start to lower your arm as you keep up that circular motion. Lower your arm (keep that clockwise, circular motion) until you are now even with your chest.

- Without stopping that clockwise motion, what direction are you going in now? Well, if you followed the directions, your motion is now *counter-clockwise*.

You started out clockwise, yet without changing your direction at all, you ended up going the opposite way. The only change was your perspective. Looking up at your thumb, you saw a completely opposite direction than when your view was at chest level.

If you are a teacher or manager, team leader, mother, father or anyone in charge of leading a group of some kind, I want you to really think about this lesson. If you are in the position of expecting results from others and you give people direction of any kind, always remember that their point of view might be much different than yours.

When I speak to students, especially the younger ones, I have to be careful when discussing the ideas of never giving up and always working hard to follow the dream. It's important to let them know that our dreams can change, that we can actually have more than one dream. This is important because as much as I wanted to get drafted by the Boston Celtics as a kid (it's still a fantasy, though), that wasn't going to happen for me. As much as I could work on a jump shot, nothing would help me become a 6'7 wing with a 43-inch vertical.

Likewise, I don't know anyone, me included, that's never played air guitar and didn't dream of being on stage in front of a sold-out crowd. In my case that was a fantasy (okay, that still is, too). But ask me how many guitar lessons I've taken over the course of my lifetime. Aside from my uncle showing me a few chords, that answer would be zero. So becoming a serious musician wasn't going to happen. Why? Because I wasn't willing to put the work in – turns out that this wasn't my dream.

Knowing the difference between the dream (a realistic goal that our students can work towards) and fantasy (enjoying lottery millions without buying the ticket) is extremely important. If our students (and us) want something bad enough, they are going to invest in themselves and do the work. But they have to be realistic.

For example, I have helped other people get their book projects off the ground by showing them how to self-publish. One person who came into contact with me wanted to know how he could make his book a New York Times best seller. Great question, right? Who wouldn't want to be a New York Times best-selling author? I told him that it takes a strong team of people doing a lot of advance work, promotion, getting reviews and creating as much buzz and presales as possible to have a shot at that kind of immediate success. But more than anything, it takes really good writing.

"What was the last book you read?" I asked him.

This is a question that usually doesn't require a lot of thought. But in this case, he couldn't remember. After some prodding, he finally came clean and explained to me that he didn't like to read at all. This response left me flabbergasted. And I recall this conversation so clearly because I was at the park with my daughters that evening and I blamed my laughter on, "something I just saw my daughter do on the monkey bars." It was no coincidence that the first draft of his story had to go through a heavy editing process – even the illustrator on the project was lost when he took a look at the first draft.

The dream was to become a best selling author but when you don't even like to read in the first place, well, this is a problem. People who write for a living ended up doing what they do because other writers inspired them. Along with some of my sports idols growing up (shout out to Larry Bird!), some of my heroes were authors. I loved the stories and journeys they took me on so much as a kid and now as an adult, that I wanted to do what they did, too. I wanted to tell my own stories. But I knew it wasn't going to happen overnight. There was going to be a lot of work involved.

I understand that there are exceptions to every rule, but wanting to be an author but hating to read is like wanting to be a heart surgeon but hating the sight of blood. It just doesn't make sense!

Applying The Second Rule to Happiness doesn't mean that every dream is going to come to fruition right off the bat. In fact, some dreams do not come true for various reasons, some beyond our control. Failure is a part of life and we have to accept this fact. I know many people, some of them very successful in their respective fields, who have failed more than most people have even tried.

If there is one topic I know a lot about, it's failure. I give my wife a lot of credit because she has heard every cool idea that I've ever had and has seen me fail at trying to act on these ideas many times.

Let's take this project, for example. In fact, let's talk about all of my writing projects. I go through a period of panic when I sit down to write something. The fear of failure has a way of reaching out and gripping me behind the neck and squeezing. Hard. Not only does that grip keep me from working, it makes me second-guess myself. It makes me worry about what other people would think. The next thing I know, I am putting off the project entirely and re-thinking the entire thing before I even start typing.

How crazy is that, right? In my head I start going through the rejection process on a manuscript that hasn't even been written yet!

But back to this project for a sec: #TheHappyManifesto is a HUGE leap from what I've previously published. I've been writing for children for the last eight years. So I wouldn't blame some people (and, ahem, acquisition editors) for wondering why I decided to cast my line and fish in another pond, so to speak. And my answer would be this: Why wouldn't I?

Seriously? Don't I offer a certain perspective as a former teacher, someone who has traveled extensively, has visited classrooms, spoken to parents and teachers? Haven't I self-published my work and leveraged those projects to traditional publishing contracts?

I'm not kidding; this is the type of pep talk I had (and still have) to give myself whenever I think I am not good enough. But I can't be my own enemy (there will be no shortage of enemies in life so why add to that total, right?). I have to push forward, find the message that I want to share and believe in it.

Push. Find. Believe.

So as we think about how we're going to convey this idea to our students, let us also think about those dreams we may have missed out on. And as we look back on what may have derailed us in the past, ask yourself why you wanted to achieve that dream in the first place. Was it a superficial reason? Maybe you were younger at the time and had no idea what it was going to take to achieve that dream? Or, perhaps you now realize that your dream was more of a fantasy? And that's okay, seriously. But as we look back, let's also look ahead knowing what we know now and find what it is that will truly fulfill us. And once you find it, start believing in it.

Start believing in you.

Understanding this in our own lives is going to help us convey this important Second Rule to our students and children. Our expectations of them are high (and rightfully so). However we should never, ever, forget that they are a lot smarter than we sometimes give them credit for. They don't need to actually *see* the pig pen to know they're standing close to it, to put it lightly.

The first two rules help our students to start believing in themselves. Being better than good helps give all of us the attitude check we need to go beyond average and rise above expectations. It sets the bar higher. It provides us with a very important perspective as we look back on missed opportunities we may have had because we weren't in the right mindset.

The First Rule of Happiness serves as a foundation for the Second Rule. When we have the right mindset, purpose and belief, we can start acting on it and working hard to accomplish our goals, no matter what.

It's important that we understand that just because we're applying the First and Second Rules, successful outcomes do not just happen over night. You see, the concept of patience has diminished in this day and age. We're so point and click that gratification needs to come immediately or we scroll to something else. Our attention spans are shorter. Therefore, people are always looking to achieve the dream but they want it very quickly, which almost forces them to skip out on the Second Rule. There's nothing exceptional or above average when we choose to take shortcuts instead of putting the work in.

Here's an example that will surely resonate with all students…

Despite all the warnings and tragic stories that you read about, there are still athletes out there (young and old) taking steroids. At my gym there's a group of guys that might think that they're fooling people. But the only people they're fooling are themselves.

All the signs are there, from the back and shoulder acne to the disproportioned bodies. But there are also some guys who are using steroids that don't fit this stereotypical profile. These are guys who are closer to middle age looking to recover from hard workouts faster, as well as to increase their energy. Essentially they want to turn back the clock and have their bodies perform at levels they may have had 20 years ago.

Rather than adapting to the bodies they have, working out smarter and more efficiently, steroid users take the shortcut, putting themselves at risk in order to reach their goals. They are actually doing the opposite of why we should be exercising in the first place – to feel good. But for this particular group of steroid users, looks take precedent.

I can't mention the "steroid bros" without also talking about the surgically enhanced glamour girls that we see from time to time. It's a little jarring to see a woman who's face is so pulled back that she looks like a cat, pawing at her phone instead of using the exercise machine that she's perched on while people wait... and wait. Listen, I'm all for trying to look good – this is a terrific byproduct of trying to feel the best we can. But you know someone's overdone it with the butt implants when her backside is still entering the gym while she scans her membership card at the front desk!

Like the steroid users, the physical appearance takes priority over what's actually going on with the body on the inside. We get healthy from the inside out, not the other way around. Just like I can spot a steroid user a mile away, I also recognize those individuals who are consistently working hard to better themselves in the gym. I see their workouts and observe their intensity. Heck, I've even learned by just watching their form and have even asked them for help.

Inspiration can come in many different ways and from those you would least expect. Several months ago an elderly gentleman in a wheelchair showed up to the gym and made a huge impact on me. He's become a regular, coming in a few times a week. A specialty bus with a lift drops him off and picks him up right at the front entrance so that he can wheel his way inside and get to his workout.

This man doesn't know it, but he pushes me just by being there. He goes about his business, adapting to machines that weren't necessarily made for someone in a chair. He exercises with the kind of intensity one would expect from a guy half his age. He's putting serious work in, striving to be a better version of himself at the end of his workout than the person who first rolled into the gym. And he gives me all of the perspective and proof that I need to know how important The Second Rule is: Always work hard to follow your dreams.

Don't ever forget that not working hard for the dream is the equivalent to wanting to win the lottery without buying the ticket. There has to be some kind of work in order to make progress. Yet, there are still people who choose to ignore The Second Rule altogether. Sure, they mean well, they want to succeed. However, they tend to have a problem with adversity, with overcoming challenges that many people struggle with – including the people that we'd consider to be successful.

So how do they circumvent this problem and avoid the Second Rule? Oh, there are plenty of ways, yet nearly all of them do not offer any kind of real growth. There are those people that choose to pay someone else to do the work for them. But where does the learning go? There is no personal development when we get others to do the work for us, an old lesson from my time in school when teachers warned us about having other kids do our homework. Many of you reading this manifesto have undoubtedly reminded your students that they end up cheating themselves. Sure, the immediate result is a high homework grade. But what happens when they have to take the test?

Students that work hard and understand that

success is not an overnight phenomenon will have a better appreciation for patience. They can accept the fact that their patience is going to help carry them through those rough stretches where it seems like they are never going to "get it." But in time that switch will eventually flip on. And that light will shine as bright as their newfound confidence!

# The Third Rule of Happiness

## #TheHappyManifesto - Three Rules for Happier Students

**I** suppose I began telling stories out of necessity rather than pleasure – I had to "come clean" to my parents whenever I got into trouble as a kid (which happened pretty often). In fact, my four brothers and I talked ourselves out of as much trouble as we got into (again, a lot). You actually have to be pretty creative to explain why the car got totaled – 10 miles away from home when you were only supposed to drive "to the corner, nowhere else or your father is going to beat the living you-know-what out of you." Anyway…

The love of reading had a lot to do with me wanting to tell stories, too. I tell students and parents that I'd dive into stories headfirst, the way a kid cannonballs into a pool on the first day of Spring Break. Opening up a book was like traveling through time and space, teleporting me wherever I chose to go. Books allowed me, a kid from West Texas, to feel the yearning desire to save my pennies, nickels and dimes for a pair of Redbone hounds (Where The Red Fern Grows), or become a sea captain chasing a giant whale or float down the Mississippi River with my friend Jim (The Adventures of Huckleberry Finn).. The stories I read as a kid had an impact on me, so much so, that eventually I knew that I wanted to try to take people on similar journeys.

But I couldn't do it alone.

As with the previous rules, the Third Rule works in tandem with its two counterparts. We know that the First Rule, be better than good, calls for us to be better than average. It allows us to raise the bar, not just for students, but also for all of us. It's an attitude adjustment. We should strive to be better than good in everything we do.

The Second Rule is about dreams – specifically it's about helping our students understand the difference between the dream and the fantasy. Always work hard to follow your dreams. Don't be the person that waits for the dream to come true or for that door of opportunity to open. Be the one that kicks open that door. As I wrote in the previous chapter, not working hard for the dream is like wishing you won the lottery without buying the ticket. It's hard to win if you don't put yourself in the game. The dreams is more prone to coming true if you're willing to put in the necessary time and effort into making it happen.

**The Third Rule** helps put everything together:

**Always be willing to help other people follow their dreams (because you never know when you'll need help with yours).**

Look, I'll be honest; if you were to ask me to draw a circle it's going to look like a potato. There's no way my books get published without the help of talented illustrators willing to adopt my projects as if they were their own and make the words come to life. My dream of telling stories, taking people on journeys, doesn't happen without their help. People, who could draw much, much better than I ever could, helped foster my dream. And in the cases of two of the illustrators I've worked with, I helped foster their dreams, as I provided them with their first book illustration gigs.

In short, it's pretty rare to achieve our dreams by ourselves. We can't go through this world alone. We need help. We need people to bounce ideas off of, people that are willing to listen and support us. I could easily fill about 20 more pages of this book just by listing every person who provided me with support of some kind.

I suppose it all started with my parents. With five boys it's pretty safe to say that they didn't have a lot of free time on their hands, especially when you have three kids in diapers – all at once. Between the changing of diapers, settling arguments (basically breaking up fights), the feedings, the clothing, the games, the practices, the emergency room visits, the attitudes, the hormones, the testosterone and everything else associated with raising five boys, my mother didn't have a lot of time to herself much less time to read to us. Bedtime stories weren't the norm, although I do remember some of them.

*#TheHappyManifesto - Three Rules for Happier Students*

What my mother did all the time (and still does to this day) was encourage us. She allowed us to use our imaginations, even if it meant looking the other way when we raided my dad's garage to steal (and lose) his shovels and other tools so that we could go build forts in the desert and pelt each other with dirt clods.

If Hollywood needed a bad guy my father would have been perfect for the role. He was a man of very few words (At his Rosary I said that he was very stingy with his words). He was the enforcer, the giver of punishment when we needed it. An imposing figure, my father could make a man turn away and run just by looking at the poor guy. But I remember how hard he laughed and how his entire demeanor could change during those times he smiled.

If kids pick up and learn through observation, than my father showed me how enjoyable it was to grab a book and read. Everywhere he went, there was a paperback along for the ride. There were books in his truck, in his lunchbox. I'd often wake up in the morning to find that he had passed out on the couch, a book resting on his chest and his reading glasses propped up on his head. My parents had a room that we called "the library" because there were so many books that he had collected over the years. Many of these books belong to me now. His love of reading definitely rubbed off me.

While I saw my father's joy of reading at home, it was an elementary school teacher that furthered my love for the written word.

Mrs. Eugenia Scott will always be one of my favorite teachers and I will forever be thankful for the gift she gave my classmates and me one afternoon at Surratt Elementary School in Clint, Texas.

I recall that day very vividly. Roughly 15 minutes before the final bell rang, Mrs. Scott told us to clear our desks. This was met with the usual sighs and "uh-oh's" and "now what's" because generally when a teacher tells a class to clear their desks, the follow-up instruction is,

## #TheHappyManifesto - Three Rules for Happier Students

"And take out a blank sheet of paper." Pop quiz!

But that didn't happen. Instead, Mrs. Scott stood centered behind a podium and looked at each and every one of us until all students had settled down. A tall woman, Mrs. Scott had a confident, smooth stride every time she walked down the halls; there was a presence about her that was commanding, yet subtle. I can't remember her yelling at us to settle down because she simply didn't have to.

"Today I am going to give you a gift," she began (still one of the best ways to get a class's attention, I might add).

Mrs. Scott went on to explain that from that day forward for the rest of the school year, she would be reading to us. Our only job was to close our eyes and imagine every word that came out of her mouth. She wanted us to enjoy the idea of being read to without worry of getting tested or quizzed or homeworked to death.

*Phillip D. Cortez, MCM*

She started with Where The Red Fern Grows by Wilson Rawls. And when she was finished with that book, Mrs. Scott took out Dear Mr. Henshaw by Beverly Cleary and gave us a new adventure to go on. I may not love reading the way I do today had it not been for her.

Mrs. Scott didn't know it at the time, but she was fostering my dream of wanting to be a writer one day.

For everyone reading this manifesto, especially those of you who are current students, I want you to think about some of the teachers you've had up until this point. Isn't it funny how the mind works sometimes? For most of us, whenever we have to go back in time and think about something like what I just asked you to do (think about some of the teachers you've had), we automatically fall into two different buckets: those who think about the good teachers who have had the most positive impact on us or those who think about the crummy teachers that clearly chose the wrong profession. Which bucket do you fall in?

For those of you that fell into the first bucket, concentrate on what it was about these teachers that was so positive. What words of encouragement did they use? What did they do to help you?

If you fell into the second bucket, you thought about the bad teachers, I want you to think about what you *wished* they had said. How did you feel after your negative experience with that teacher? What actions could that teacher have taken to help better support you?

No matter what bucket you fell in, action must be taken. If you were in the group that thought about the positive teachers, you must now pay it forward and be a positive force for someone else.

If you were in the second group and had thought about the bad teachers in your life, you now need to think about the outcome you really *wanted* to experience but didn't. You now need to remember that moment of disappointment and frustration the next time you are in a position to help. Because if you don't, that cycle of negativity will never be broken, right?

In both cases, you must now execute The Third Rule, which is to help foster the dreams of others.

Teachers, good or bad, are not the only ones that are in a position to provide immediate help for the students they teach and coach. Fellow students can be that shining light we desperately need when it gets dark on us. As an example of this I make it a habit to mention one particular former classmate of mine, Marco C. Saenz, whenever I talk about The Third Rule in front any type of audience. In high school, Marco would never be accused of being the most vocal kid in our class. He did a lot of his talking through his incredible illustrations, instead. I tell people that Marco's skill was beyond his years as a teenager.

I'll never forget the day some of the guys in class erased a homework assignment that our poor History teacher unsuccessfully tried to hide on the chalkboard by pulling down a projector screen. In the time it took our teacher to walk roughly 25 feet from where he was standing outside between bells, Marco drew the teacher dressed in a sparkling Elvis Presley jumpsuit, complete with pork chop sideburns, microphone and platform shoes.

From the moment class began we couldn't wait for the instructor to reveal our "homework assignment." And although the look on our teacher's face was hilarious (he even had to laugh and admire Marco's handy work), what really stood out to me was how nonchalant Marco was about the whole thing. He seemed to be embarrassed with all of the attention he received, as news of our little stunt quickly filtered throughout the school and the rest of the student body.

If someone would have told me back then that Marco would be fostering my dream of publishing a children's book one day, that he'd be bringing my words to life, I would have never believed it.

My story is certainly not unique. As someone who has met countless business owners, I find it so refreshing to learn that many partners that went into business together were once classmates. And in many cases, they were classmates from the time they were knee-high to a wastebasket.

I think about how I may never would have met Marco had it not been for the Mexico City earthquake of 1985, one of the most devastating on record in which thousands lost their lives. Marco told me that as a result of this natural disaster, he and his family were forced to move north to Ciudad Juarez, located right on the US-Mexican border next to El Paso, Texas. The move allowed him to attend Cathedral High School in El Paso, a private Catholic school for boys. The rest is history.

So how does this translate to the lives of our students? For starters, we need to understand that it's not only the adults that can help foster our dreams. Our inspiration, our help, can come from anywhere. You might be a student sitting in your homeroom class right now reading this (good for you!) and there could be three or four of your fellow students who might be there for you down the road – and right now.

In our schools across this country and the world, young people find themselves locked in an environment where everyone is going through constant physical and emotional change. Testosterone levels are rising while hormones are bouncing off the walls. Teachers and students in this environment are navigating through an emotional minefield, it seems. If our words carry a lot of weight, imagine how heavy our words are for people locked into this environment during this time of physical and emotional development?

I asked a middle school student what it would feel like if someone laughed at his dream.

"Like crap," he replied to laughter.

"We'd give up and settle for less," another young woman responded.

Think about that for a moment. What if we all gave up and got used to settling for less? Where would we be; what would our businesses, schools and communities at-large be like if this was how we operated? You can't necessarily set educational or business goals with this way of thinking.

The simple truth is that when we put someone down or make fun of his or her dreams, well, isn't this a form of bullying? Yes it is. You see, usually when we think of bullying, we think of flying fists, schoolyard fights or worse. But we often forget how much weight our words carry. And the voices of negativity are all around us, from the halls and office buildings to the comments on our social media posts.

I remember a kid laughing at me when I told him that I wanted to write books one day. That was way back in Mrs. Scott's class. That kid laughed at me. I remember how much that laughter stung. So I kept this dream a secret all the way through high school.

Consider the following scenario…

A fifth grade student shares with her class her dream of becoming a professional soccer player one day. She hears the following comments from her classmates:

- "Uh, yeah, suuure."
- "You? Professional?"
- "You know they run a lot in soccer, right?"
- "You should maybe think of something else."

Imagine how this makes the girl feel hearing all of this from her classmates. And I think many of us have been there before, whether we've witnessed this type of verbal abuse or we've been on the receiving end of it. Heck, maybe we've even taken part in this behavior.

As bad as this might sound coming from

classmates, imagine how much worse this abuse would be for the little girl if it came from her parents? I mean, our parents are supposed to be the very first people in our lives that believe, that foster, that support and love, right? So if this little girl's parents are saying these things, what do you think will happen? More than likely, she'll start believing them! Sooner or later, this fifth grader's dream of becoming a professional soccer player will fall by the wayside.

When students apply The Third Rule, this little girl hears something different, something more positive:

- "You'd make a great soccer player."
- "My team can use another player."
- "We should play at lunch."

The same thing happens when adults begin to apply The Third Rule.

- "Let's find you a team."

- "Why don't we kick the ball around after you finish your homework?"
- "We should watch a live match one day."

Essentially, it doesn't take much for us to begin helping people achieve their dreams. In fact, we don't have to be an expert. If a kid wants to play soccer professionally, it's not a requirement that we played on a team once. We don't have to know who the starting midfielder is for the Columbus Crew much less know what being off sides in soccer means in order for us to help. We can help by listening, encouraging and connecting.

When we listen to someone, we're giving that person our time. And we all know that time is valuable. Most people have a difficult time finding someone who is willing to listen to them, especially in this day and age. You'd be surprised at how much value you provide another person just by listening to them.

Words of encouragement are important to hear, especially when someone starts to feel down or experience self-doubt. Remember, our words carry a lot of weight. This is where we can essentially make or break a person. And we have a choice to make: are we going to build someone up or are we going to tear someone down? If we are applying what we've learned so far, we are building, contributing to our own and someone else's happiness. If we're better than good we're going above and beyond with our words when fostering someone's dream.

When we choose the other path we do not build, we destroy. Our words will help destroy someone's confidence, someone's psyche and ultimately, someone's dream.

Connecting is important, as well. I might not know how to play soccer, but I have an opportunity to connect this girl with someone who does. Better yet, I might know a coach that I could introduce this little girl to. I can provide the girl's father with that coach's phone number. In other words, when we connect, we provide some kind of value. We might not have all the answers and we certainly might not be able to help everyone out, but if we can give them something to gravitate to, something they can build on, than we've done our part in applying The Third Rule.

The scenario above is not exclusive to what some people go through in the working world, whether it's an office setting, out in the field delivering packages or selling insurance. There are those people who choose not to settle in their jobs, those who aspire to climb up the ladder, whether it is money or ambition that drives them. You may personally relate to this scenario. Imagine if you heard comments like these from your fellow co-workers:

- "You just don't seem like principal material."

- "You think you're better than us?"

- "You think you're going to be my boss now?"
- "I don't think you have what it takes."

Now let's apply The Third Rule:

- "You've been here long enough to know how to operate this place in your sleep."
- "If there's someone who knows what it takes to make this place go, it's you."
- "Here's a link to a web site that will show what classes you need to take to become a school administrator."

Every boss or manager was an entry-level employee at some point. Every principal at a campus was a first-year teacher. I remember when my cousin Teresa taught at a small private Catholic school in El Paso, Texas for very little money. But she had a passion for that school and the students attending there. Teresa stayed much longer than a typical teacher would before moving onto pursuing more schooling and eventually obtaining a Doctorate in Education.

Today she has mentored and taught many doctoral students at The University of Texas – El Paso and has seen them walk across the graduation stage in their robes and doctoral hoods. It's not the happiness and relief I see on the graduates' faces that I notice, it's the pride in Teresa's face that embodies The Third Rule. And the coolest part about this experience is that there was once someone who had a very similar look on his or her face when Teresa walked across that graduation stage for the very first time, too. It's a cycle of happiness.

Outside the world of academia, I emphasize the The Third Rule to people from the public and private sectors and how they can apply it in their daily professional lives.

For example, I deal with media sales professionals all over the globe and they face the same challenges, must reach similar kinds of goals and sell similar products. Geography makes no difference. As a consultant to these men and women, I tell them that they must position themselves in the right way. Essentially, they must take a page from The Third Rule and help small business owners grow their businesses. After all, have you ever met a business owner that strives to go out of business? I didn't think so. So essentially, these are the perfect people to apply the Third Rule to, as it's a pretty safe bet that business owners are actively working hard towards their dreams.

So I encourage these sales professionals to almost forget they're trying to get a contract signed by selling solutions for their respective media companies (That's like telling the car salesman to not sell a car.). Instead, I encourage them to position themselves with a more consultative approach and ask more questions. Rather than going through a traditional customer needs analysis, they have to be prescriptive and point out areas where a small business could be losing market share and revenue to competitors.

Here's an exercise we go through when we're talking about positioning. I provide these sales pros with two different ways to begin a phone conversation. They have to tell me which approach makes the most sense to them:

1. "Hi, It's Phillip with PDC Media. Is your marketing manager available?"

2. "Hi, it's Phillip with PDC Media. I'd love to show what your competitors are doing to grow their market share and their revenue. If you have time tomorrow afternoon, we can idntify what makes these businesses so successful and replicate this, too."

If you chose Option 2, you win a shiny cool prize! But seriously, let's break this scenario down. Sales professionals are in a perfect position to help. But they are often too focused on having to meet sales quotas. What if they focused instead on solving problems? This would allow them to sell without selling. They'd be applying The Third Rule because, as we just realized, these business owners are working hard for their dreams. They just might not be doing the best job at executing. Rather than trying to sell something (and bring about the negative perceptions that people might have about salespeople), the true challenge for salespeople is convincing their prospects that they need help. And we tend to allow consultants to help us – not necessarily sellers. So rather than showing their sales prospects a price list, I encourage them to provide immediate value to these business owners. This positions a salesperson as a consultant that grows business - not sells solutions or devices or plans. You are fostering the dream of that business owner!

As an added bonus, applying this Third Rule allows these sellers to be seen as valuable people that help businesses grow. They are now difference makers or thought leaders. They become trusted.

The same value-added philosophy works in so many scenarios that we encounter in life that the topic deserves a manifesto on its own. For example, going on job interviews will never be the same if you apply The Third Rule. Why? Because you can now position yourself to add value to the company rather than focus on selling yourself with experience and education. The tables turn when you realize that the applicant isn't the only person in that interview that has a need (the job). But the organization needs to fill a position, too. We forget that as applicants, right? So what do we do? Fill their need! Apply The Third Rule and help that organization realize it's potential! Foster that hiring manager's dreams!

The examples have illustrated how The Third Rule can be applied in different professional scenarios outside of school and home. But our focus here is on happier students and children. And, yes, The Third Rule certainly works with our students in the classroom and it definitely can work with our children at home.

Here's a story even my own kids don't know…

Dating my wife was like pulling into a drive-thru one day and ordering a #5 combo meal, extra fries and a McFamily on the side. As a divorced mother of two adorable kids, you could say that I signifiicantly super-sized my life for the better. However, it wasn't all Brady Bunch, blue skies and canned studio audience laughter while the end credits rolled. It was tough, gut-wrenching at times. It's bad enough when a guy gets love sick for a girl but in my case you'd have to triple those feelings.

Winning over those kids did not mean replacing their father. This is a losing proposition. Winning over these kids meant that I had to take a page from sales and marketing days: I had to position myself as someone who provided them added value.

"You see kids, there's your mother, your father and me," I remember saying. "If your dad is the ice cream and your mom is the chocolate syrup, think of me like that extra whip cream we spray in our mouths when nobody's looking."

Did it work? It worked for them, I think they ended up getting bribed with sundaes out of that little conversation. But, in essence, I was telling them that I was that added extra bit of support they could rely on whenever they wanted or needed it, no questions asked. Over time, I think it took a lot of pressure off of them (I know it took a lot of pressure off of me).

Here's the coolest part to all of this, though: in my quest to be that value-added piece in their lives, I am a better father and overall happier person today because of Ivan and Cameron Castillo. Along with their mother, they fostered my dream of being a father long before I ever realized I would have biological kids of my own. It will never be about how many books I have written or sold - my biggest accomplishment has and will always be my wife allowing me the opportunity to help raise those two kids.

Whew - deep breath, right?

There's a potential downside or pitfall we might

face as we're trying to help others fulfill their dreams. After all, we're only human. We could find ourselves a little envious when those people we helped actually start succeeding. And that's normal. I know what it's like to work hard for something only to see someone else find immediate success. How about you? Stop for a moment and think about a time you had a great idea, only to see someone else act on it first.

In high school I was hopeful of playing quarterback for my freshman team, even though I was about 125 pounds soaking wet and no helmet was small enough to fit my head. But the coaches decided to entertain me (and themselves) any way. I worked hard during summer two-a-days, learning the offense, lifting weights (barely), all while hoping to go through a growth spurt so that I could be like my older brother, Steve, a man-child whose shoe size and age were the same (13), could bench a small car and run through defenders like a tank. As for me? Well, it didn't take a genius to figure out who got the football genes in the family.

But I was determined. And then this tall, lanky kid showed up to practice one day. His name was Mack, a good football name. He seemed to know some of the guys on the field. After some stretching, Mack picked up a football and began tossing it to another kid right next to me. Turns out he was a quarterback, too. And for about 20 seconds, we were locked into a tough quarterback competition. All it took was for him to throw one pass to an open receiver and my days as a quarterback came to an end right there. I knew it, the coaches knew it – even the little kids swinging on the monkey bars across the street knew it.

Did my pride take a hit? Sure, it stung for a little bit. But I hung in there, deciding to play wherever the coaches wanted me to play. I could have chosen to stay envious, pout, or display a bad attitude. I could have treated Mack poorly. I could have quit right then and there.

Instead I chose to be his wide receiver - I'd be on

the other end of those passes in practices and games. More importantly, I got to know him better and, as it turned out, we had a lot in common. For starters, our parents used to double date when *they* were kids. Our mothers were pregnant with us at the same time. It turns out that I was two weeks older than Mack (the only race I'd win against him).

Mack became my best friend. Heck, he became my brother. And I shudder to think of all that I could have missed out on had I taken a different path. All the fun, all of the stories, the hanging out, the trouble we got into and out of from the age of 14 to now, almost 30 years since that summer day at Ponder Park throwing the football around gone forever. Erased. I don't even want to think where my life would be today.

When we help other people with their dreams, we're also letting go of any envy or jealousy that we might experience. Any thought of "That should be me" dissolves when we're sincere in helping someone else achieve a goal. In essence, we're able to let go of that negativity because we're now responsible for making someone happier. This, in turn, should make us happier people, too. Like our teachers and professors do at yearly graduation ceremonies, we should take pride in the success of others, especially when we played a part in that success.

The Third Rule could almost be broken into two separate rules, 3A &3B. Or maybe we should just look at this rule as two sides of the same coin, heads and tails. The heads side is what we can do to help foster the dreams of our students. But the tails side of this coin is how willing they need to be to actually accept help when they need it. The Third Rule helps teach them the importance of having an open mind.

Let's think about this for a moment. How many of us have been narrow in our approach to working towards our dreams? How many of us have actually needed help, but didn't know how to ask for it? Or worse, how many of us had too much pride to ask for that help? After all, you could be applying the first two rules but spinning your wheels if you're incapable of asking for help, right?

Sheela Wolford, a former instructor at UTEP who taught a media writing class, turned out to be a gift from above as it pertains to my development as a writer. She took a look at a homework assignment of mine at the beginning of the semester and decided to make a phone call to a friend of hers, who just so happened to be the sports editor at the El Paso Herald-Post. I'll never forget that day.

I was in a classroom full of students and Sheela was handing out papers that we had turned in the previous session. Once you heard your name, Sheela allowed you to leave for the day. Once I heard my name called, I began to make my way to the front of the class. That's when she stopped me in my tracks.

"Phillip I'm going to need to see you after class,"

she said.

I heard students collectively ooh and turn my way in laughter. I was embarrassed but tried not to show it. I felt people staring…

After the last student left, that's when Sheela had told me about the opportunity to go and work as a part-time contributor at the evening newspaper. Whatever it was she saw in my assignment, Sheela decided that my work was good enough to put a good word in on my behalf. That afternoon I was hired at the paper. And the very next week I found myself on the sidelines working as a legit reporter at the Sun Bowl, as the Dallas Cowboys were scrimmaging the old Houston Oilers.

Then a funny thing happened - seeing my work in the newspaper everyday while still a student totally inflated my ego. And long before there were children in my life to keep me humble - Is that a white nose hair, daddy?! - there was Dr. Barthy Byrd, one of my professors at UTEP. She pulled me aside one day and told me that she wanted to see me in her office. *Gulp*.

I remember this as if it were yesterday. There wasn't a cloud in the clear, blue sky and it was still early enough in the spring to where the El Paso sun wasn't punishing anyone who dared to be outside.

I knocked on her door and stepped in her office. On her desk was a stack of newspapers and other assignments she had not yet graded. It hadn't dawned on me that the newspapers on her desk were all turned to pages where my stories appeared.

Dr. Byrd took out a red marker and proceeded to go over articles that had already gone through the editing process and printed for public consumption at a daily newspaper! She pointed out areas where I sounded too passive, where I could have used better words. She challenged me to re-write some of these stories.

What does a 20-year-old know? If you ask most of them, the answer is EVERYTHING. Dr. Byrd was making me better at a time when I thought I didn't need to be. I thought that having my work in print was the finish line in the writing process. For Dr. Byrd, she made sure that I understood that the learning never stops.

You may have experienced similar scenarios with your students. We can't let them make the mistake of thinking that asking for and accepting help is a sign of weakness. On the contrary, it takes a lot of character and integrity to understand that you may have reached a limit in your efforts to work hard to achieve your dream. This is why we have coaches, right? We need guidance. And how can you help someone else when you aren't able to get help for yourself? Here I am all these years later and I'm still thanking my lucky stars that there were people like Sheela Wolford and Barthy Byrd that crossed my path!

Getting help doesn't have to pertain to our professional lives, either. The Third Rule plays brilliantly in our personal growth, as well. My wife has been so instrumental in this department. I mentioned before that she has heard every idea, every fleeting thought or project or business that I wanted to pursue, look into and (more often than not) fail at. This woman has seen me fail so much more than I have ever succeeded. She's seen me at my worst; she's seen me at my best. She's still with me, keeping me in check and making sure that I don't float away like a helium balloon in the wind. She is always there holding that string so that I don't float away.

And I love her for it.

The Third Rule allows us to take the dreams of our students and children and help them hold onto those balloon strings so that they do no float away. It allows us to help those dreams grow, whether we're listening, encouraging or connecting.

We're also teaching our kids the importance of humility, to be willing to accept help from others. They need to understand that when someone is willing to help in some way, they must gravitate to them, learn from them and hold them close by making them a part of their tribe. Our students can certainly work hard for the dream – but they do not have to go through their journeys alone.

In fact, none of us have to.

# Putting It All Together

*#TheHappyManifesto - Three Rules for Happier Students*

**B**y now we know that The Three Rules for Happier Students is a three-step cycle in which all three work in tandem, feeding off one another and repeating over and over again. The Three Rules, when applied, radiate beyond the classroom and onto others. Your positivity is like clean sheets from the dryer, it's refreshing as you go about your day, never settling for average and working hard.

Meanwhile, people begin to take notice. Our students are seen as people who can be counted on, thought leaders, people who help by listening, encouraging and connecting. Others begin gravitating to them. Their confidence skrockets!

When we apply these rules outside of academia in our every day jobs, we see referrals increase, people begin to see your strengths; they begin to envision you as part of their team. Being better than good has raised the bar, your goals are higher than other people's goals, and that means you work harder than they do. You're willing to help others whenever possible but at the same time you are open to being helped. You're open to learning from others, too.

And the cycle repeats.

Can you see how that when we focus on these Three Rules we naturally eliminate outside distractions? We now have the ability to stay more focused, more centered and forward thinking in our attempts to reach our goals? We can rise above the trivial and petty office or school gossip. How awesome would it be if we all applied these rules into our every day lives? How different would things be for us if we just gave ourselves and our students a solid foundation to work with?

I'd say there'd be a lot more positivity in our immediate vicinities. The shortage of happiness that I wrote about in the beginning of this manifesto would be fully stocked. And there'd be a never-ending supply for each and every one of our children, our students and everyone else to consume and share. We can make our lives, the students we teach, our children and those around us better, happier.

But it all starts with being better than good – to ourselves and to each other.

**Phillip Dominic Cortez** became fascinated with books and stories at a very early age. It wasn't long before he wanted to write his own stories.

"I was always making up stories to try and get out of trouble anyway," he laughs. "But that sort of comes with the territory when you've got four brothers."

Cortez holds degrees in Organizational Communication/Public Relations from the University of Texas - El Paso and a Masters of Communications Management from the University of Southern California. He still loves to read and, with his wife, Patty, is now fascinated by the many stories told by their four children: Ivan, Cameron, Ava and Zoe.

## Speaking & Workshops

From corporate events, professional development and school readings at every grade level, I thoroughly enjoy participating in and adding value to events across the country. I'd be honored to take part in your next event. Simply visit www.phillipcortez.com and fill out the form today! I'll cater my message to any audience in order to help your organization meet its goals.

# Acknowledgments

I'd like to thank the following people for helping out on this very different, yet important, project of mine: Becky Calderon, Sheela Wolford, Julie Franco, Dr. Teresa Cortez, Emily Francis, Bertha Arsola, Andrea Darby and Rosie Rodriguez. Thank you for the support and feedback you provided!

Notable teachers and mentors also include Eugenia Scott, Louie Saenz, Robert Candelaria, Dr. Henry T. Ingle, Dr. Barthy Byrd, Leo Cancellare, Brother Nick Gonzalez, Dr. Connie Kubo Della-Piana, Sister Jennifer Marxer & Dr. Daniela Baroffio.

Infinite thanks to my parents, Salvador & Irene; my brothers Steven, Michael, Paul and Mark - you guys have been here from the beginning. Bobby and Cathy Rosales for being second parents to me; brothers from another mother Robbie, Paul and Mack. My wife, Patty, and our children are always with me, whether I'm working from the kitchen table or from some strange airport terminal - thank you & I love you!

Lastly I want to thank all of the teachers and students that I have had the pleasure to speak to over the last eight years. You guys are amazing! Teachers, my hats off to you for the wonderful work you do! I look forward to visiting more of your classrooms and libraries in the near future!

www.ingramcontent.com/pod-product-compliance
Lightning Source LLC
LaVergne TN
LVHW051128080426
835510LV00018B/2302